W9-AGB-642

VOICES of GETTYSBURG

VOICES *of* GETTYSBURG

By Sherry Garland
Illustrated by Judith Hierstein

PELICAN PUBLISHING COMPANY

GRETNA 2010

ACKNOWLEDGMENTS:
Special thanks to the personnel of Gettysburg National Military Park and to
Capt. Dave Bock, Ohio Valley Civil War Association.

*The word "Pelican" and the depiction of a pelican are trademarks
of Pelican Publishing Company, Inc., and are registered in the
U.S. Patent and Trademark Office.*

Library of Congress Cataloging-in-Publication Data

Garland, Sherry.
  Voices of Gettysburg / by Sherry Garland ; illustrated by Judith Hierstein.
    p. cm.
  Summary: Relates, through illustrations and short passages, events of the Civil
War Battle of Gettysburg and its aftermath as seen through the eyes of soldiers,
from generals to privates, as well as various civilians. Includes historical notes.
  ISBN 978-1-58980-653-5 (hardcover : alk. paper) 1. Gettysburg, Battle of, Get-
tysburg, Pa., 1863—Juvenile fiction. [1. Gettysburg, Battle of, Gettysburg, Pa.,
1863—Fiction. 2. United States—History—Civil War, 1861-1865—Campaigns—
Fiction. 3. Pennsylvania—History—Civil War, 1861-1865—Fiction.] I. Hierstein,
Judy, ill. II. Title.
  PZ7.G18415Voi 2009
  [Fic]—dc22

                                    2009003963

Printed in Singapore
Published by Pelican Publishing Company, Inc.
1000 Burmaster Street, Gretna, Louisiana 70053

JUNE 3, 1863

I am Gen. Robert E. Lee, commander of the Army of Northern Virginia,
seventy-five thousand of the finest young soldiers
who ever dedicated themselves to a cause.

Today we begin the northwestward march to Pennsylvania.
It saddens me to leave Virginia, my beloved homeland,
but the enemy has ravaged her towns and fields
until there is nothing left here for this army to subsist upon.
Across the Potomac River the lands are fertile, the storehouses full.
Once the North has tasted the bitter harvest of war like the South
and suffered a sound defeat in her own valleys and hills,
perhaps then her people will pressure Lincoln for peace.

My army is outnumbered by the Army of the Potomac.
We are outgunned by their better weaponry; they are better supplied;
but time and again my ragged soldiers have faced this enemy and won.
The Federals will try to stop us with all their strength,
but I have confidence in my courageous boys in gray.

All the hopes of the Confederacy rest upon this campaign.
With victory, soon this cruel war will be over.

JUNE 13, 1863

I am a private in the Second Wisconsin, Meredith's Brigade.
For many days rumors have been flying that the Johnny Rebs
bivouacked across the Rappahannock River from here are moving out.
The Allen brothers with their observation balloon counting tents and campfires
tell us that the Army of Northern Virginia is vanishing like morning dew.
Some think General Lee is shifting his troops to Vicksburg
to bust up General Grant's siege on that Mississippi town.
Others think he's going to invade the North again.

Our scouts still don't know where the crafty old gray fox is located,
but yesterday we received orders to strike camp and move north.
None of us want to face Lee's army again, not after the beating our boys took
at Fredericksburg and Chancellorsville just a few weeks ago.
But, by Henry, if they trespass on our homeland,
they'll soon find out why we're called the Iron Brigade.

JUNE 27, 1863

I am Rachel Cormany, of Chambersburg, Pennsylvania.
This morning my babe and I awoke to the strains of
"Dixie" and "The Bonnie Blue Flag" under my window.
All day long the Rebels tramped by,
thousands upon thousands,
cheering and waving their state banners with glee,
hauling frightful artillery and an endless trail of wagons.
Such a rough, dirty, raggedy set one does not often see!
They are poorly clad—many have no shoes.

An officer asked me if he might buy some bread for his men.
He said General Lee had ordered them not to plunder,
to respect the citizens and pay for every item.
But the Confederate dollars he offered
are as worthless as dirt.

JUNE 29, 1863

I am Gen. George Meade, new commander of the Army of the Potomac.
Yesterday morning at 3 A.M., I was rudely awakened in my tent
by an official sent from President Lincoln to inform me that
I am now in charge of this army of over one hundred thousand men.

The Army of Northern Virginia has invaded Pennsylvania;
the Union army is making a grueling march trying to find it.
I do not like the idea of going against General Lee,
the officer who served the United States so honorably for years,
but President Lincoln has ordered me to protect Washington
and to crush the secessionist army no matter what it takes.

General Buford's cavalry is scouting north of here
hoping to find the location of the Confederates.
I do not know exactly where or when it will come,
but a battle will soon decide the fate of our nation.

JULY 1, 1863
Morning, Day One of the Battle

I am a private in Fry's Thirteenth Alabama, Archer's Brigade, Heth's Division.
We got up before dawn full of vigor and excitement.
Rumors flew that we were marching into a town called Gettysburg
to find a warehouse filled with fine new shoes.
I hoped it true, for I have walked barefoot many a day.

The only Yankee soldiers in town were supposed to be local militia
or a little cavalry that we'd be able to whip faster than a fox.
Through misty rain and silver fog we tramped down Chambersburg Pike
until we were about three miles west of that little town.

Without warning, Yankee cavalrymen on foot stood up
and commenced firing with carbines and Colt revolvers.
For two hours we pushed them back, through the fields and over a hill.
At a little creek, more Billy Yanks popped up from the bulrushes,
and their light artillery began screaming at us from a ridge,
their canister shot spewing deadly metal all around.
We fought like bobcats for another hour, then suddenly we saw
the woods ahead swarming with thousands of Union infantry.

"This here ain't no local militia," shouted my sergeant.
"This here is the Army of the Potomac."

JULY 1, 1863
Evening

I am John Burns, citizen of Gettysburg, seventy years of age.
When word came that the rebellious army was advancing,
I picked up my flintlock musket and powder horn
then walked to the battlefield to offer my help.

In McPherson's Woods, I fought beside the Iron Brigade,
those determined warriors in their strange black hats.
Soon more Rebs arrived from the west and the north.
They were everywhere—at the creek, on McPherson's Ridge,
at the barns, at the railroad cut, in the roads and fields.
Thankfully, more boys in blue arrived to give them battle.

There were small victories and many losses on both sides,
but alas, at the end the Rebels overran our boys on Seminary Ridge.
Retreat was sounded, with our cavalry galloping through town.
The Union soldiers regrouped on the hills and ridges south of here.

I heard someone say that Union casualties are extremely grave,
but now our boys have possession of the high ground
and are fortifying it well.
The Confederate army will have to pay dearly to get that ground.
We are temporarily defeated, but this battle is not over yet.

JULY 2, 1863
4:30 P.M., *Day Two of the Battle*

I'm a private in the First Texas, Robertson's Brigade, Hood's Division.
We got ready this morning for an assault on the ridges
where the Yanks ran off to yesterday evening after they got whipped.

We advanced until we saw those dern Yankee signalmen
perched on top of a bald, rocky hill
itching to wig-wag their red and white flags
and tell ol' General Meade where we were heading.
We marched miles out of the way to avoid being seen.

By four o'clock we were exhausted and out of water.
I was hungry enough to eat a skunk
when we finally got the order to attack.
We took heavy fire, fighting tooth and nail
'til we came to a huge jumble of granite boulders,
some as big as a barn, with Yankees on the summit
firing down at us with everything they had—
grapeshot, canister, sharpshooters—
cutting us down like stalks of wheat.

I prayed to God and Momma and our ol' dog Blue,
promising I would mend my ways if I'd just get
through this day alive.

JULY 2, 1863
Evening

I am Col. Joshua Chamberlain, once a college professor
but now commander of the Twentieth Maine Infantry.
My orders were to protect a rocky peak called Little Round Top,
where our signal station sat—a spot of great advantage.
I positioned my men on the woody slope
and opened fire as the Confederates attacked.
We repelled them, but they charged again and again
with their chilling Rebel yells.

My men were almost out of ammunition;
we could not hold back another charge.
So I gave the order to fix bayonets
and we stormed down the hill, through the trees,
running with such fury that we took them by surprise
and we held that piece of barren rock.

Now the second day of battle is over; thousands lie dead.
In the end, nothing was gained nor lost.
Both the Union and the Confederate lines
remain where they were when the day began.

JULY 2, 1863
Night

I am Sallie Myers, a schoolteacher of Gettysburg come to this church
to help care for the wounded and dying soldiers in blue.
They began arriving yesterday after the first fighting,
bearing the most ghastly, horrid wounds.
They filled the churches, then the barns, warehouses,
private homes, and pitched white tents.
The groans of agony are almost too much to bear.
The sight of the surgeons covered in blood,
tossing amputated limbs out windows,
makes my stomach turn.

The wound dressers long ago ran out of gauze,
so women of the town bring any cloth they can spare.
The wounded beg for water and the dying
give me their possessions to send back home.
I hastily write down their final words,
promising them I will tell their wives or mothers
or sisters or sweethearts that they died like men.

I will cry tomorrow; I do not have time to cry today.

JULY 3, 1863
3:15 P.M., *Day Three of the Battle*

I am a color-bearer in General Armistead's Virginia Brigade, Pickett's Division.
Orders came for a frontal assault on Federal lines entrenched on Cemetery Ridge.
We waited for hours in sweltering heat, sweat trickling down our backs.

Around 1:00 P.M., Confederate cannons commenced firing at the foe.
The Yanks responded by firing their cannons right back at us.
For two hours the earth shook; our ears ached from the deafening roar.
It was impossible to speak or hear your own pounding heart.
Thick smoke filled the sky, stinging our eyes; shattered tree limbs fell all around.
When the cannons stopped, General Pickett rode before us and cried out:
"Charge the enemy. And remember Old Virginia!"

Drums rolled a steady beat as we formed up shoulder to shoulder.
There are to be no Rebel yells or running until we are almost there.
We must cross open ground for almost a mile before we reach Union lines.
General Armistead, off his horse so he will not be an easy target,
put his hat on the tip of his sword as a sign for us to follow.

Surely our heavy cannonade destroyed the Federal artillery. Surely it did.
If not, then we are sitting prey and may God have mercy on our souls.

JULY 3, 1863
4:30 P.M.

I am a gunner in Battery B, First New York Light Artillery.
The Johnnies bombarded us with cannonade for two hours this afternoon,
but their projectiles went long and did little damage to our fortifications.

After the cannons went quiet, I could not believe my eyes.
Here came over twelve thousand Rebs in perfect formations across the open fields.
Our artillery opened fire, mowing them down from three directions.
They rallied 'round the flag and kept coming, still in silence,
but when they were close, they let out their Rebel yells and charged.
We fired with everything we had. They wavered and stumbled,
but still they kept coming, what was left of them.

They reached the stone wall at the foot of Cemetery Ridge,
behind which thousands of the Union line were waiting.
At an angle in the wall, the blood ran in streams
as men fought viciously and desperately.
At last, the shattered Rebels sounded retreat,
leaving half their men on the field.

There was no point in pursuing them;
surely the human soul cannot endure another day like this.

JULY 4, 1863
Early Morning

I am Alfred Waud, artist for *Harper's Weekly* magazine,
hired to record the deeds of this war in pencil and ink.
As I look upon the fields strewn with the dead and dying,
littered with broken limbers and caissons,
abandoned muskets and dead horses and mules,
I can hardly bring myself to draw this ruin and sorrow.

The ambulances and stretcher-bearers
work swiftly to remove the groaning wounded,
while the burial crews begin their grisly task.
Gravediggers mark the bodies of Union soldiers
with pieces of fence board for later burial at Cemetery Hill.
For the Rebel dead, they dig long trenches and toss them in
without ceremony or tear shed.

I saw a Union driver weeping over the body of a Rebel.
   I asked him why he felt pity for a soldier
      who had brought such grief to our nation.
         "He was my brother," the man sadly said.
            "Nothing else matters than that."

Plymouth Center School
Library Media Center
107 North Street
Plymouth, CT 06782

JUNE 1872

I am with the Ladies Memorial Association of Richmond, Virginia.
When our brave Confederate sons fell at Gettysburg,
they were thrown into unmarked trenches
and called traitors and followers of an immoral cause.

So ladies in the South took up collections
to pay for the return of our dead.
Not long ago the remains of those gallant boys
who fell at Gettysburg arrived
to be interred in the warm Southern soil.

Sad faces lined the street as the solemn procession
passed by to the sound of a funeral dirge.
At last the fallen will rest in peace and honor,
at last they will have flowers laid
and tears shed over their graves.
Though most of the headstones
be marked "Unknown," it does not matter,
for at last they are home.

GETTYSBURG DEAD

JULY 2, 1923

I am a war veteran from Georgia, come here one final time
to see these grounds where I lost my youth and innocence,
where I watched my comrades fall sixty years ago.

There aren't many of us left now, and the young folk
do not care about our stories of courage, of fear, and of death.
They have their own stories of the Great War
when Northern and Southern boys fought side by side
with no memory of Gettysburg to cloud their heads and hearts.

I climbed on top of this rocky hill; it was no easy chore.
I saw another white-haired man resting on his cane.
"I was there at Devil's Den," he said.
From his accent I knew he fought for the Union side.
"And I was there, too," I replied.
"Maybe your Minié ball was the one
that makes me walk with a limp," he said.
"And maybe your Minié ball was the one
that took my two fingers," I said, showing my hand.

He smiled and so did I, then we embraced
as if we were long-lost brothers.
Maybe we were.

HISTORICAL NOTE

The Battle of Gettysburg had the greatest number of casualties of any battle during the American Civil War and has often been called the war's turning point. Yet it was by accident that the battle occurred near the sleepy Pennsylvania town of Gettysburg on July 1-3, 1863.

By 1863, the American Civil War had been raging for more than two years. No one had expected it to last so long and to be so costly in human lives and property. Much to the dismay of Pres. Abraham Lincoln, the Confederacy was not only putting up a gallant defense, but it also had soundly defeated the Union armies in several major battles, the two most recent being at Fredericksburg and Chancellorsville. This success was unexpected, since the industrialized North had a much larger population from which to draw soldiers as well as a larger army with better weapons and better supplies.

In the Virginia area, where the majority of battles took place, the Union army was called the Army of the Potomac, commanded by Gen. Joseph Hooker. The Confederate army in that region was called the Army of Northern Virginia, commanded by Gen. Robert E. Lee. In the spring of 1863, these two large armies were camped across from each other in Virginia, with the Rappahannock River running between them.

In May 1863, Lee devised a plan that he felt would end the war favorably for the war-torn South. He would invade the Northern states, forcing a major battle that he was confident he could win. If the Northern states had to suffer invasion like the South had, there was a good chance that the strong antiwar movement in the North would bring pressure on President Lincoln to negotiate for peace. And since Virginia had been ravaged by the war, Lee wanted to move his army to a place where food and supplies were more plentiful. Lee also hoped this plan would cause the Union army to abandon its siege of Vicksburg, Mississippi, farther west. Too, a victory might bring much-needed foreign support to the Confederate cause.

The Army of Northern Virginia began quietly moving out on June 3, 1863, traveling west over the Blue Ridge Mountains, then north along the Shenandoah Valley, across the Potomac River, through Maryland, then into Pennsylvania. The cavalry, which was the eyes and ears of the army and commanded by Gen. J. E. B. Stuart, was to monitor the Union army movements. At first,

Union generals were at a loss as to what Lee was planning; some even thought he was moving his army west to save Vicksburg. It was not until June 12 that General Hooker finally gave orders for the Army of the Potomac to move north, where rumors of a Confederate invasion had been flying for days, creating a panic.

Union soldiers marched north at a grueling pace, not knowing exactly where Lee's army was located. President Lincoln was so disappointed with General Hooker that on June 28, he appointed a new commander for the Army of the Potomac, Gen. George G. Meade. Meade was given orders to find and crush Lee's army and to protect Washington, D.C.

By June 28, part of Lee's army was massed at Chambersburg, Pennsylvania, about twenty-five miles west of Gettysburg. Another part of Lee's army, led by Gen. James Ewell, was near Harrisburg, Pennsylvania, poised to attack that unguarded capital. That night a Rebel scout informed Lee that the Union army had crossed the Potomac and was in Maryland, not far away. A shocked Lee, who had not yet heard from his cavalry, immediately recalled Ewell's corps, deciding he would make a stand on the hills near Cashtown, about eight miles west of Gettysburg. But first he had to reunite his divided army.

Still unaware of the whereabouts of Lee's army, Meade thought the battle might occur in Maryland. He sent cavalry brigades north seeking information about the location of the Army of Northern Virginia. With two cavalry brigades, Gen. John Buford arrived at Gettysburg on June 30. Citizens told him that large numbers of Confederates were massing at Cashtown. Realizing that Gettysburg was a good strategic location, with roads radiating in all directions, Buford sent word to the nearest Union infantry, commanded by Gen. John Reynolds, asking for reinforcements. Buford began fortifying the areas west and north of town with his troopers on foot rather than on their horses. They hid behind tall grass and rises. He also set up light artillery on a ridge. Buford kept a wary eye on his men from the cupola of a Lutheran theological seminary.

General Lee had ordered his generals not to engage the enemy until he gave the command; he wanted the entire army concentrated in one place before he fought a battle. However, on June 30, Third Corps commander A. P. Hill gave permission to a division general, Henry Heth, to go into Gettysburg the next day.

Some say he wanted shoes; others say that is a myth. Although Heth expected little resistance, he took an entire division of seventy-five hundred men and field artillery.

The Battle of Gettysburg was about to begin. It was not one specific battle on a single day, but many simultaneous battles fought over a three-day period.

On July 1, the first day of battle, Heth's Confederate division marching toward town ran into one brigade of Union cavalry. The Confederates slowly pushed the cavalry back one mile. Soon both Union and Confederate infantry reinforcements arrived. They fought at McPherson's Ridge, the Railroad Cut, and McPherson's Woods. At the end of the day, Confederates took Seminary Ridge, forcing the Union troops to retreat through town and regroup on hills south of Gettysburg. That night, thousands more reinforcements arrived for both sides.

On July 2, the second day of battle, Lee ordered a morning attack, but several delays prevented the assault from occurring until about 4 P.M. By that time the Union troops had set up fortifications and artillery on more hills. The Confederate forces met stiff resistance in locations called the Wheatfield, Devil's Den (a mass of huge boulders), the Peach Orchard, Big Round Top, Little Round Top, the Slaughter Pen, Cemetery Ridge, Trostle House, and Culp's Hill. This was the bloodiest day for the Union. At the end of the day, there was no decisive victory for either side, though the Confederates came close to taking the high ground.

At Meade's headquarters the Union generals argued over what to do. Some wanted to retreat, others wanted to make a stand. It was decided that they would stay. Lee also consulted with his generals. He wanted to make a frontal assault on the Union forces on Cemetery Ridge. Gen. James Longstreet disagreed with Lee's plan but in the end followed orders.

On July 3, the third day of battle, at 1 P.M., Confederate cannons on Seminary Ridge opened fire and bombarded the Union line on Cemetery Ridge. Union cannons responded. The air turned white with smoke and the roar was deafening. Unbeknown to the Rebel cannoneers, the projectiles were firing long. The two-hour barrage did little damage to the Union artillery.

Meanwhile, three miles east of the battle, J. E. B. Stuart's cavalry, assigned to attack the Union right flank and rear, ran into Union cavalry that included a daring twenty-three-year-old Gen. George A. Custer. The delay prevented Stuart from achieving his goals.

Around 3 P.M., the Southern cannons ceased. In what is called "Pickett's Charge," between 12,500 and 15,000 Confederates marched toward the center of the Union line, across one mile of open ground. Union artillery devastated the unprotected men, but the soldiers in gray kept advancing. Fighting was especially deadly at the foot of Cemetery Ridge where a rock wall cut an angle. In less than an hour, most Confederate regiments had lost over 50 percent of their men. Seeing the hopelessness of it, General Pickett called the retreat around 4 P.M. As the survivors limped back, General Lee himself rode among them, consoling the weary soldiers and taking the blame.

On July 4, both sides started collecting their wounded and burying the dead. Estimated losses for the three-day battle were staggering. Union casualties included 3,155 killed, 14,531 wounded, and 5,360 captured or missing. Confederate losses were 4,708 killed, 12,693 wounded, and 5,830 captured or missing. Many of the wounded died later, making the death toll even higher. Total casualties for the six-week-long Gettysburg Campaign are estimated at over 57,000 killed, wounded, or missing.

That evening, in a blinding rainstorm, the Army of Northern Virginia began its retreat. Lincoln wanted General Meade to immediately pursue Lee's army and crush it, but Meade hesitated. When Lee's army came to the swollen Potomac River, they discovered the pontoon bridge had been destroyed, so they used two small flatboats to carry more than 10,000 wounded soldiers across even as engineers built a new bridge. Then the rear of Lee's army was attacked. Many were killed or captured, but the Army of Northern Virginia survived to fight another day. The war continued for two more years. Total deaths for the entire war were over 620,000.

In November 1863, at the dedication of the Soldiers' National Cemetery at Gettysburg, Pres. Abraham Lincoln gave his famous address to honor the Union dead. The Confederate dead lay in unmarked mass graves until 1871-73 when ladies memorial associations in several Southern cities raised money for the removal and reburial of the soldiers in Southern soil. Today Gettysburg National Military Park stands as a reminder of the sacrifices made by the brave men who fought and died those three days in July 1863.

GLOSSARY

BIVOUAC—a temporary encampment or shelter, typically using tents

CAISSON—a two-wheeled vehicle for carrying extra artillery ammunition

CANISTER—a tin can full of metal balls, fired from a cannon

CARBINE—a short-barreled, lightweight rifle; Sharps was a famous brand

CAVALRY—troops mounted on horseback

COLOR-BEARER—the person who carried the unit's flag

DIRGE—slow, mournful music, often played at funerals

INFANTRY—soldiers who travel by foot; all officers rode horses

LIMBER—detachable cart with ammunition chest, hooked to front of gun carriage

MILITIA—hometown military units formed to protect local areas

MINIÉ BALL—a cone-shaped bullet that expanded when fired

PONTOON BRIDGE—temporary bridge held up by floating supports

SIGNAL CORPS—unit that used flags, torches, and telegraphs to convey information

SELECTED BIBLIOGRAPHY

Bicheno, Hugh. *Gettysburg*. London: Cassell & Co., 2001.

Gallagher, Gary W. *The First Day at Gettysburg*. Kent, OH: Kent St. University Press, 1992.

——. *The Second Day at Gettysburg*. Kent, OH: Kent St. University Press, 1993.

——. *The Third Day at Gettysburg and Beyond*. Chapel Hill: University of NC Press, 1994.

Pfanz, Harry. *Gettysburg: Culp's Hill and Cemetery Ridge*. Chapel Hill: University of NC Press, 1993.

——. *Gettysburg: The First Day*. Chapel Hill: University of NC Press, 2001.

——. *Gettysburg: The Second Day*. Chapel Hill: University of NC Press, 1987.

Reardon, C. *Pickett's Charge in History and Memory*. Chapel Hill: University of NC Press, 1997.

Symonds, Craig L. *American Heritage History of the Battle of Gettysburg*. NY: HarperCollins, 2001.

Tucker, Glenn. *High Tide at Gettysburg*. Old Saybrook, CT: Konecky & Konecky, 1958.

Wert, Jeffry D. *Gettysburg, Day Three*. NY: Simon & Schuster, 2001.

SUGGESTIONS FOR FURTHER READING

Andrews, Harris J., ed. *Gettysburg*. Vol. 2 of *Voices of the Civil War*. Alexandria, VA: Time-Life Books, 1995.

Clark, Champ. *Gettysburg: The Confederate High Tide*. Alexandria, VA: Time-Life Books, 1985.

Clasby, Robert. *Gettysburg: You Are There*. Short Hills, NJ: Burford Books, 2003.

Deangelis, Gina. *The Battle of Gettysburg: Turning Point of the Civil War*. Mankato, MN: Capstone Press, 2006.

Hynson, Colin. *The Battle of Gettysburg*. Grand Rapids, MI: School Specialty Pub., 2006.

McPherson, James M. *Gettysburg*. Atlanta, GA: Turner Publishing, 1993.

Murphy, Jim. *The Long Road to Gettysburg*. New York: Clarion Books, 1992.

Smith, Carl. *Gettysburg 1863: High Tide of the Confederacy*. Westport, CT: Praeger Publishers, 2004.